TOGETHER WE STAND:

A Northern Alberta Wildfire Story

Matthew Marcone

&

Jordan Maskell

Liberty Multimedia Inc.

Copyright © 2019 Liberty Multimedia Inc.

All rights reserved.

This document is geared towards providing exact and reliable information in regards to the topic and issue covered. The publication is sold with the idea that the publisher is not required to render accounting, officially permitted, or otherwise, qualified services. If advice is necessary, legal or professional, a practiced individual in the profession should be ordered.

In no way is it legal to reproduce, duplicate, or transmit any part of this document in either electronic means or in printed format. Recording of this publication is strictly prohibited and any storage of this document is not allowed unless with written permission from the publisher. All rights reserved.

The information provided herein is stated to be truthful and consistent, in that any liability, in terms of inattention or otherwise, by any usage or abuse of any policies, processes, or directions contained within is the solitary and utter responsibility of the recipient reader. Under no circumstances will any legal responsibility or blame be held against the publisher for any reparation, damages, or monetary loss due to the information herein, either directly or indirectly.

ISBN 9798602936469

Cover Design by pro_ebookcovers

Printed in Canada

Published by Liberty Multimedia Inc.

217 Royal Elm Road NW. Calgary, Alberta. T3G5V5

matthew.marcone@gmail.com

jordan_maskell@live.ca

Edited by Maire E. Train

www.libertymultimedia.com

Table of Contents

Introduction 1

Chapter 1 : Just Another Wildfire 6

Chapter 2 : Town Of High Level Evacuated 15

Chapter 3 : A Supporting Cast Stays Behind.................. 24

Chapter 4 : Controlled Burn Operation Creates Containment Boundary... 37

Chapter 5 : The Calm Before The Storm & Paddle Prairie Metis Settlement 46

Chapter 6 : Fire Growth & Residents Return To High Level 58

Chapter 7 : Mandatory Evacuation In La Crete 64

Chapter 8 : Paddle Prairie And La Crete Residents Return Home 71

Chapter 9 : The Chuckegg Creek Wildfire: Being Held 81

References 91

INTRODUCTION

Northern Alberta, Canada is home to a massive, remote land area providing thousands of people with unique opportunities. Situated in Canada's Boreal Forest, the region's abundant resources create livelihoods for dozens of municipalities, remote communities and traditional landholders, who thrive on a vast array of boreal wildlife, forestry, agriculture, oil and natural gas resources.

This is the story of *The Chuckegg Creek Wildfire* of 2019, and how it is forever changing the region encompassing High Level, La Crete, Fort Vermilion and surrounding Indigenous communities of Bushe River, Meander River, Chateh, Beaver First Nation and Paddle Prairie Metis Settlement.

At its peak, Alberta Agriculture and Forestry were measuring this deadly fire beast at over 351,800 hectares in size – ripping through huge areas of forest, destroying 14 houses, millions of dollars in structural and industrial equipment, and provoking mandatory evacuations throughout the region.

Through interviews with dozens of community members who stayed behind, firefighters on the front line, first responders and other volunteers, we've been collecting, editing and archiving stories to try and capture the magnitude of this truly phenomenal event. As a company and team with strong ties to the Northern Alberta region, these stories are 100 per cent local and inspired by the same question many people were asking during the heart of the evacuations: "How can we help?"

As professional multimedia publishers, this is our answer to that question. It is the result of eight months of research and collaborating with many of the people at the heart of this story, all of whom we owe a huge thank you.

While it would take nothing less than a remarkable team effort to pull through, there remains an emotional healing process taking place throughout the north. Some are reporting mental health related trauma including youth diagnosed with Post Traumatic Stress Disorder (PTSD), and it is our hope that through telling this story, it will provide people with a better understanding of what happened, some level of entertainment, and maybe even help in the healing process.

Paddle Prairie continues suffering the greatest losses, where 14 houses and 60,600 hectares of forest – or nearly 35 per cent of the Settlement's boundaries – are eviscerated. A rebuilding effort is underway and fortunately, there have been no reported deaths. As the wildfire continues smoldering underground throughout the winter of 2019-20, there remains a heavy anxiety throughout the region.

Beyond the tragedy of this event, there exists a more inspiring narrative involving an unprecedented multi-regional cooperation. New friendships are formed, opening up better opportunities for the future.

We are electing to release the First Edition of this book in black and white, and are also offering this story in colour as a one-hour feature documentary available at www.libertymultimedia.com. We will then be submitting this movie to numerous film festivals in order to get this story seen throughout the province, country and world. In the event you or your business/organization would like to play a role in this mission, while having your brand forever associated with the project, please contact libertymultimediacanada@gmail.com or Matt/Jordan at 780-247-1625.

We hope you enjoy this book and can take something valuable away from it, whether you are a resident of the area, or simply looking to learn more about one of the largest wildfires in Alberta's history.

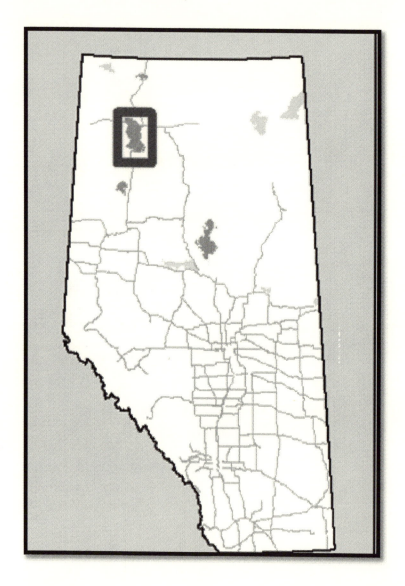

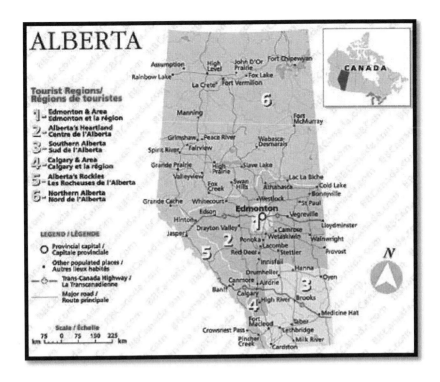

A visual look at northern Alberta, labeled #6 in this 2001 Map by Government of Canada. This book tells the story of the 2019 Chuckegg Creek Wildfire encompassing High Level, La Crete, Fort Vermilion and surrounding Indigenous communities of Bushe River, Meander River, and Paddle Prairie Metis Settlement. At its peak, the fire was 351,800 hectares in size, or more than 657,000 football fields!

CHAPTER 1

Just Another Wildfire

"Fire HWF042, started on Sunday May 12, 2019 and is located 23 km south, of the Town of High Level. This fire was previously classified as 'Being Held' (BH) but due to gusty winds out of the southeast this fire is back to being classified as Out of Control (OC) at 1,817 hectares. In result of the high winds, the fire experienced activity on the north and northwest side of the fire perimeter. There is no threat to the community of High Level."

Alberta Agriculture and Forestry High Level Wildfire Update: May 12, 2019

Northern Albertans are no strangers to wildfire threats, which are a natural part of the forest cycle. They are typically caused by human activity, with dry lightening also being a major contributor.

Over the last few years, these events appear to be increasing in severity. The well-documented 2016 Fort McMurray wildfire ended up becoming the costliest disaster in Canadian history, with damages exceeding $9.8 billion, forcing upwards of 88,000 people from their homes and destroying over 2,400 structures.

In 2011, a wildfire racing through Slave Lake eviscerated over 400 homes and buildings. Zama City also evacuated in 2012 over a memorable wildfire scare.

To the north, residents of the Northwest Territories are seeing an increase in wildfire severity as well. This peaked in 2014 with 385 wildfires burning throughout the territory – 57 per cent above average. Extreme weather events are being exacerbated by hotter and drier climate conditions, which scientists are expecting to continue in the years ahead.

The 2019 wildfire season appeared no different for residents of northern Alberta. A May 17 wildfire update from Alberta Agriculture and Forestry was tracking a small wildfire south of High Level, which did not initially appear to be a threat.

"You know we thought, 'Ok it's a fire on the edge of the highway and the wind was pushing it across the highway, but we stopped and talked to Forestry,'" said Town of High Level Fire Chief Rodney Schmidt. "They were working it and we headed home. As we do in every season, we kept in close contact with Forestry so we knew what was going on with the fire and it was actually looking good through the week."

"Everything changed on Friday the 17th when things really picked up in terms of wind," Schmidt continued. "And that's when we had another fire that evening east of Town where a power line came down and threatened a structure. We went out with Forestry, Fort Vermilion and La Crete Fire Departments and we managed that fire there, and we could see on the horizon *The Chuckegg Creek Wildfire*. We got back and contacted Forestry and they said 'it's making a run.'"

Within one day, the wildfire had grown from 1,817 hectares to 25,334 hectares and residents were taking notice.

"People were watching this fire for four or five days," explained Crystal McAteer, Town of High Level Mayor. "They could see that it was inching its way towards High Level. They could see the smoke. They were taking pictures. It was shared throughout social media long before we told them to get ready."

Back at his home in High Level, Schmidt could see the plume of smoke getting higher and higher on the horizon.

"We went out to the Forestry office for a flight and took a look at the fire," said Schmidt. "And as soon as we got up in the air, I knew we were in trouble. I said on the intercom as we were flying, 'this thing has got a mind of its own.' It was doing things that we haven't seen in a long time, and I've been doing this for a while and the fire behavior was very active. All you could do is do your best to kind of steer it the best you can, and when it's wind-driven like that, there is just nothing you can do."

An aerial view of what would become known as The Chuckegg Creek Wildfire. Photo supplied by Rodney Schmidt.

"I could see it in his face," McAteer said after meeting with Schmidt. "When he told us that he thought we should probably start preparing, that's when I started to get a little alarmed. The first thing I did was call my daughter and say 'get ready to evacuate within 72 hours.' And of course, those visuals are in your mind. I watched the Fort McMurray fires and people fleeing through walls of flames, trying to get their horses out, and everything that goes along with it. Slave Lake had a relatively short period of time to get out of town, so I didn't want our people to have to experience that."

With the wildfire approaching, Town of High Level began assembling teams, beginning with communications and setting up an Emergency Operations Center (EOC). The EOC is the primary municipal response to an emergency. The Incident Command Post – or ICP – also started managing the operations and responding to the tactical side of the emergency.

"We don't have the T.V. media that they have in the big cities," said McAteer. "I mean if they were in the cities they would be monitoring that fire with helicopters, it'd be all over the news. There would have been reporters out there watching this fire. Social media was a good medium at that point because a lot of people shared, re-shared and so that message got out."

Mackenzie County simultaneously started their emergency preparations over the weekend, which was off to a slow start on account of staff being away for a major conference being held in Quebec.

"I thought about it quite a bit and I made the decision to bring everybody back," said Len Racher, Chief Administrative Officer for Mackenzie County. "That took a little while. Carol Gabriel, she jumped on a plane right away. Byron Peters, all our key people were on route back and then the perfect storm started to hit."

Having experienced the worst of northern Alberta wildfires, the first people that Town of High Level called for help were the fire crews in Slave Lake.

"They've been through this," said Schmidt. "We helped them in 2011 and we've worked with them countless times on many fires threatening communities across the province in the past several years, and our teams work really well together. They had a crew on the road the next morning. We also called Clearwater County [and] a team up here called Alberta Task Force One."

Alberta Task Force One was co-founded by Schmidt with the help of many fire chiefs and fire service personnel in Northwest Alberta.

"A group called the Peace Region Fire Chiefs built this incident management team with Albert Emergency Management Agency and it's the first time this team has ever been tested," said Schmidt. "They've been training for two years and when I talked to the mayor and Clark on Saturday, I said 'we need to bring the team here. We need to let them manage this event for us. We don't have enough people in our town staff to fill this massive flowchart that we are about to build to manage this event.' And they immediately agreed."

By Sunday, May 19, Alberta Transportation closed off Highway 35 south of High Level, as well as Highway 58 to the west. The threat becomes so severe that it is officially named *The Chuckegg Creek Wildfire*.

"We had a lot of smoke behind the greenhouse," said Alexandra Barreira, Co-owner of Sunscape Gardens, a greenhouse just north of High Level. "There was lots of dark smoke, lots of clouds. We didn't know where it was coming from, how close it was, we couldn't see because there are so many trees behind our property. We didn't think it was going to hit us, until we saw the smoke up on Watt Mountain there, then things got a little intense."

In addition to Barreira's regular duties owning and operating the greenhouse, she now had a new routine walking to her neighbour Kelly Wilde's place to see whether the fire was getting any closer.

"I always felt like we were fine here, because for the fire to get to us it has to burn through town first," said Barreira. "That's going to take time to do, so I never really thought about the fire coming from the west. I thought Footner Lake and all that swamp was there, never realizing that it does burn through that swamp quite fast too."

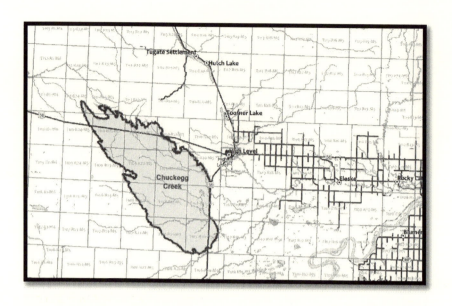

The Chuckegg Creek Wildfire is a mere 3km from Town of High Level on Monday, May 20, 2019. Map courtesy of Alberta Agriculture and Forestry.

CHAPTER 2

Town of High Level Evacuated

The Chuckegg Creek fire has grown due to strong winds, and is now approximately 69,000 hectares. This fire is located approximately 3 km south of the Town of High Level and remains classified as Out of Control (OC). Warm temperatures and high gusty winds are forecast again for today; in result the fire has been experiencing increased fire activity.

The Town of High Level has issued an Evacuation Order for the town as of May 20, 2019 at 4:00 p.m. Evacuations will be carried out by zones, within town limits. Residents are recommended to secure their residences (lock doors and windows) take any personal belongings (pets, identification, medication, small denomination of cash, etc).

Alberta Agriculture and Forestry High Level Wildfire Update: May 20, 2019

By Monday, May 20, fear was gripping the entire region. *The Chuckegg Creek Wildfire* was now roaring out of control at

69,000 hectares and sitting just 3 km from High Level, threatening to wipe out the entire town.

As emergency resources were arriving, a mini-command center was established inside High Level Fire Department. This allowed the Town to better organize all of the resources that were coming in so quickly.

"At 4 a.m. we got a call from Norbord that the fire was 1 km or less from the plant," said Schmidt. "And that's when everything went from, I would say bad to worse at that point. I pulled everybody together after the power went out in the morning and I said, 'this is the real deal. You need to take some time now and contact your families and let them know that there is likely an evacuation coming.'"

"We have always talked to our firefighters in the past that when something threatens the town, your families are going to leave and you're going to stay," Schmidt continued. "And so we said, 'now is the time to have that talk and make sure that you guys are prepared for what's about to come, because this isn't going to get any easier over the next few days.'"

The Chuckegg Creek Wildfire is less than 1 km from Norbord – a major lumber producer in the region just south of High Level – on Monday, May 20, 2019. Photo supplied by Rodney Schmidt.

Town of High Level's Chief Administrative Officer Clark McAskile said that by 6:30 a.m. on Monday, May 20, it was clear to everyone involved that Town of High Level would be evacuating. The mandatory evacuation was officially issued for residents south and southeast of the Town of High Level at 11:40 a.m.

"We were getting concerned just because every night as the winds died down the fire spread," said McAskile. "It widened, and the winds picked back up the next day continued to push the fire toward Highway 58. So then we were trying to organize an evacuation without power and without communications in some cases."

There are two power feeds that service Town of High Level, one of which comes from Paddle Prairie to the south and the other from Rainbow Lake to the west. Operations Supervisor for ATCO Electric George Fehr explained how *The Chuckegg Creek Wildfire* managed to take out both those feeds during the evacuation day.

"The fire came through and burned up trees and the right of way, and ultimately the poles caught fire," said Fehr. "So the line falls down and we had a bunch of damaged infrastructure from that, and so we had to put all the poles back up."

"And of course, the fire was very active," Fehr continued. "So once we had the one feed restored and we thought we could turn it back on Monday, the fire circled back and took up more poles on that feed. That's why the outage was prolonged; the fire did more damage as we were repairing from the south. We did everything we could to get the power back on and I think it was an effective response."

With Town of High Level under mandatory evacuation, fire crews are hard at work and doing everything they can to protect life and structures. Photo by Jarrett Austin.

Chief James Ahnassay and Council for Bushe River – a neighbouring Dene Tha' First Nation – also issued a mandatory evacuation for community members on Monday. Others in places like Chateh were voluntarily evacuating on account of heavy smoke; in particular elders, kids and people suffering from respiratory conditions.

Meanwhile, Mackenzie County continued scaling up their efforts in anticipation of all the evacuees who would be heading east away from High Level.

"We lost power. We lost cell service," said Racher. "The fire was heading towards the towers. With the power out, they only last three to five days on battery, and then it was too dangerous to get up there to put generators up. So everything just started escalating huge, so we did [too]. We went big, fast and hard. We just kept getting bigger and bigger and bigger accommodating all those evacuees. We were assisting with everything from security to helping with road closures. The RCMP and School Board were awesome because they stayed there with us."

Mike McMann, Superintendent for the Fort Vermilion School Division, said their staff was working tirelessly with RCMP to run security 24/7, while also ensuring people would have a nice place to sleep. For others like Schmidt, the evacuation of High Level brings back eerie memories.

"People were honking their horns at us, just waving and saying, 'thank you and good luck,' and it was just really odd," said Schmidt. "My wife called and she said, 'I'm at the fire hall, meet me there,' so I came down and saw her. We had all kinds of stories of families that were completely disrupted so people could stay. So we said our goodbyes and I said, 'we'll see you in a few days,' because everybody thinks it's going to be a few days, right? Like this fire is going to go by us and everything will be fine. But it wasn't, it wasn't even close."

In six hours, Town of High Level had successfully evacuated approximately 4,000 people.

"What I found interesting as part of that evacuation plan is [that] on Sunday and then early Monday morning, they were already phoning people and saying, 'hey we'd like you to stay,'" said McAskile. "That would not have occurred to me. To me, an evacuation is you get everybody the hell out of dodge."

For Tony Barreira, Co-owner of Sunscape Gardens, the biggest focus was keeping everyone busy so they would not panic.

"I know my kids were panicking there for a while and we had a fellow with us that was quite concerned and panicky too," said Barreira. "So keep everybody busy because as long as they are busy, they are not thinking about the fire."

"I started making up fire hoses," Barreira continued. "I made 1000 feet of fire hoses, three splits so that I could tee it off into three different places. Altogether we were putting out a 6 1/2-horse pump and it was fairly steady. I actually built two fire nozzles that I could shoot water from one side of the greenhouse right across to the other side, just so that we could make sure that we kept the whole roof watered."

The Barreira family was among a steady group of people preparing to stay behind for as long as possible.

"We were practicing with the fire hose because we thought, 'well we have to be prepared to fight this fire,'" said Alexandra Barreira, nervously recalling those moments. "I wasn't going to leave until I absolutely had to."

Alexandra and Tony Barreira of Sunscape Gardens practice with a fire hose, and are getting ready to fight The Chuckegg Creek Wildfire. Photo courtesy of Sunscape Gardens.

CHAPTER 3

A Supporting Cast Stays Behind

"The Chuckegg Creek Fire remains approximately 3 km south of the Town of High Level and is classified as Out of Control (OC). Due to current conditions and resources the fire has not reached the Town of High Level. The main area of spread remains on the northwest side of the fire, away from town. Firefighters along with air support from helicopters and air tankers have been focusing efforts on the east side of highway 35 and continue to be effective.

Fire activity and smoky conditions make it challenging for firefighters to get an accurate GPS of the fire perimeter. When this issue arises Alberta Wildfire uses aircraft to do a high-level aerial scan at night. Data from the scan will be collected in the morning and new size will be determined. The last recorded size is approximately 79,805 hectares."

Alberta Agriculture and Forestry High Level Wildfire Update: May 21, 2019

While fire crews, heavy equipment operators and emergency responders were out on the front lines, a team of local volunteers elected to stay behind to function as a supporting cast.

"I asked if I could just stay around longer in case things changed," said Jan Welke, Owner and Pharmacist at High Level IDA. "And I'm glad I did because within the next day – with the power being out as well – we were starting to get requests from the public for prescriptions and for items and some were panicky, 'how am I going to get this, how am I going to get that?' Some of this messaging was coming through Facebook even, so even on the first day, we were busy filling prescriptions for people."

"And I knew that if that was day one, it was only going to get more challenging as the days went on because we're quite a busy pharmacy, and we have a lot of people to serve and not everybody left far away to where there's another pharmacy. They're on the fringes of the evacuation zone; they are in the communities that weren't affected."

Sherry Matthews, Owner of Traditions Café and Gifts, said her family's escape plan was to simply drive east towards Fort Vermilion and see what happens.

"My husband pulled in a generator and started drilling a hole in the wall, just so we could have power, keep our products and things like that," said Matthews. "Then we had a friend text us – The Malmquist family – and they said, 'hey if you need a place to come, come on out.' And we looked at each other and said, 'I guess we're going to the Malmquist's house.' We knew we had to stay close because my husband works at the hospital."

The Northwest Health Centre in High Level functions as the primary hospital in the region, covering an enormous land area populated by over 19,000 people, including surrounding First Nations reserves.

Director of Clinical Operations for Area 1 with Alberta Health Services, Angie Mann, said their team of 16 – including physicians, nurses, protective services, a kitchen supervisor and maintenance – stayed behind to provide care to emergency personnel in the area. They were able to evacuate the entire hospital in approximately two hours.

"We remained open for emergency services 24/7, as well we had our operating room team on standby for any potential emergency surgeries for the area or surrounding communities, such as C-sections or really anything on an emergency basis," said Mann. "It was really informative for all of us actually to spend a lot of time on the roof and to watch the bombers and ignition specialists, and watch all the fire activities from the roof. It was a perfect seat actually."

"A look at The Chuckegg Creek Wildfire from the roof of the Northwest Health Centre in High Level. Photo by Angie Mann.

At this point, *The Chuckegg Creek Wildfire* was threatening the Town in nearly every direction.

"On Monday, I went up to go fill up my truck at UFA and there was a lineup of 10 vehicles there," recalled Malcolm Gunson, Water Treatment Plant Operator 3 for the Town of High Level. "The fire really boxed us in there for a while. You couldn't go south, you couldn't go west [and] you couldn't go north. You could only go east."

The influx of people heading east provided a big opportunity for residents of Fort Vermilion to help in any way they could.

"When High Level got evacuated, Fort got really busy," said Charles LaForge, Owner at Fantasy North Golf Course & RV. "I think my first thought was 'Ok, where are we going to put them all? We need to accommodate.' So I started running some extra wires in the campground, so there would be more outlets, more plugins for people. And I think a lot of them ended up here because they really didn't have any place to go down south."

Councillor for Mackenzie County Cameron Cardinal said that initially, many people in Fort Vermilion were feeling upset because they knew their community was safe from the wildfire, yet it seemed like they were getting bypassed.

"They were sending people to High Prairie, Slave Lake, to other communities in the south," said Cardinal. "But then all of a sudden, it was like, 'you guys have two hours to get ready, and there could be up to 500 people coming.'"

Cardinal quickly coordinated with Mike McMann of Fort Vermilion School Division and Dave Schellenberg to begin putting things together and waiting for buses to arrive.

"We put all the cots in the arena and then we were using the hall to feed people," said McMann. "I made a bunch of calls to some teachers to say, 'hey come and help out,' and in no time we had 30 or 40 people that were there assembling and moving and mobilizing the center. Most of the people in the first round came from Bushe, Chateh and Meander River. There were a few people that went to La Crete but there was a time in Fort Vermillion where we were close to that 600 mark of people living at the center. We just tried to make it home."

Staff members from High Level Native Friendship Centre Society were also playing an active role at the Fort Vermilion evacuation site.

"It's been quite the experience too for us, because we are working with people who are dealing with the trauma of the whole situation," said Melanie Badour. "We had quite a few staff members that did provide basic necessities; essentials, pampers, soap, shampoo, stuff that we had in our own center, so they gave that out during the evacuation. So even though yes we were evacuated, a lot of the staff members were still able to do what we do, and help who we help during that time."

North of High Level, another 300 residents evacuated Meander River on May 21 after the fire destroyed its surrounding power lines. While ATCO was working tirelessly on restoration, the supporting businesses and people staying behind also faced major challenges from limited communications.

"I just didn't really take the threat of evacuation perhaps very seriously initially because I've been here 30 years now, and we've had fires in the past and never before have we been evacuated," said Tareq Morad, Owner/Operator of Morad Hospitality Management in High Level. "There were a number of hours where I kind of lost total communication with anybody. I didn't know are there 50 people coming, are there 100 people coming, and for how long? They came and said we need about 120 hotel rooms."

Morad's staff operates five hotels in High Level with approximately 400 rooms in total. He said they started the evacuation with a staff of 13, which grew to over 40 in the days ahead.

Others like Sherry Matthews were already coming back into Town to check on their businesses.

"Tuesday morning we came back in, because I'm thinking we've got this big pile of diesel sitting out behind our shop," said Matthews. "I thought 'that's kind of flammable' so that was on our mind. We just didn't know how close that fire was, so we wanted to come back into town and just make sure."

While at Traditions, Matthews immediately noticed they were one of the few places in town with power. Upon offering to help, she was immediately asked to cook for 200 people.

"It was very humbling because I have a fabulous staff but I have a lot of young girls, and it's a lot of responsibility to ask them to come back to work, keeping them safe and making sure their parents are okay," said Matthews. "People are anxious and nervous. Sometimes when that's going on you don't want them to work, so the fact that these other people just volunteered and helped is overwhelming. It's hard work. Like we were in washing dishes for hours on end, because we're a small operation and in order to cook for 200, it's a fair bit of moving things around, lots of dishes. And the fact that they just stepped up. It gets very emotional when I think about what those people did."

Co-owners at Tim Hortons in High Level – Paul, Leslie and Jared Snyder – were also witnessing the most impactful period of their restaurant's history. They said most of their team members wanted to stay and were volunteering left and right.

"It was beyond anything that you could expect to have, to have that opportunity [to stay behind]," said Leslie Snyder. "Serving people in a time of extreme stress and some people say danger... we never felt in danger. That was an honour. Hearing their stories and just having that extra couple minutes in the evening when firefighters would come in and just talk about how things went. One day a mother came in and said that her son had to get in this truck, they'd been given a two-minute warning to leave an area, and she described how her son got in the truck and was going to follow another truck through a wall of fire. A wall of fire burst up in front of him and he had to physically drive his truck through a wall of fire to get out. To share those moments and the mom had tears in her eyes, I had tears in my eyes then and now. It's so powerful."

A look at the walls of fire seen as first responders are making last minute evacuations from The Chuckegg Creek Wildfire. Photo by Josh Lambert.

"Another evening a couple of guys came in and they also had been given a very short period of time to evacuate,"

Snyder continued. "They were on dozers and the fire had done a little jumping and was right beside them and they really had to almost run for their lives and leave millions of dollars of equipment right there in the middle of a fire."

For Jared Snyder, he was most impressed by their team's willingness to stay behind, even while *The Chuckegg Creek Wildfire* was raging just 3km from Town.

"That was super heartwarming because it was a scary time, a lot of uncertainty and people were volunteering left and right," said Jared Snyder. "It really was a massive team effort by everyone that was able to stay, and I think that's kind of part of like what it's about to live in the north. We don't have all this stuff at our fingertips and up here we have to rely on each other a lot. I know that this is one of the biggest fires in Alberta's history, so it just makes sense for everyone to be working together."

The restaurant effort behind the scenes was one less thing for emergency responders to worry about during the crisis.

"All I heard that week was from the people that stayed back behind, all we ever heard was 'what do you need?'" said Schmidt. "It was never a complaint. We had no power and we had this like amazing food showing up to the fire hall for 100 guys and girls to say 'here you go, just eat.' And I'm like 'how do we get 50 pizzas when there's no power?' But it just shows up."

"Had we not had those restaurant services, I have no idea what we'd have done. We would have ended up robbing convenience stores and living off cliff bars and beef jerky," joked McAskile.

A small victory took place on May 22 when ATCO temporarily restored power to Mackenzie County, Town of High Level, Fort Vermilion & Dene Tha' First Nation. The smoke on this day would be so severe that Paddle Prairie Metis Settlement Council and their Administration team would voluntarily evacuate approximately 300 vulnerable members, mostly to Grande Prairie, Peace River, and High Prairie.

By this point, *The Chuckegg Creek Wildfire* was nearly 100,000 hectares in size, and still raging right on High Level's doorstep.

The Chuckegg Creek Wildfire as May 23, 2019, sitting approximately 3 km from Town. Map courtesy of Alberta Agriculture and Forestry.

CHAPTER 4

Controlled Burn Operation Creates Containment Boundary

Today, firefighters continued a controlled burn operation to create a containment boundary along highway 35 south of High Level, and west along highway 58, as conditions allowed to do so.

Alberta Wildfire firefighters in conjunction with municipal firefighting resources, along with air support from helicopters and air tankers continue to focus containment efforts around the fire perimeter south of High Level. With current weather conditions firefighters continue to be effective, due to lighter winds out of the northeast. This in result continues to aid crews on further protecting power line poles west and south of the Town of High Level. The main area of spread remains away from town.

Heavy equipment has been working along the northeast side of the fire and continues to make progress on consolidating a guard around the fire perimeter. They have built approximately 8 km of containment line. There are 154 structural firefighters that continue to establish and maintain structural protection on homes in the

Town of High Level and on other critical values at risk within Mackenzie County. Alberta Wildfire has 143 firefighters along with 28 helicopters on this fire. There are more resources arriving daily.

Alberta Agriculture and Forestry High Level Wildfire Update: May 23, 2019

With Town of High Level, Bushe River and Meander River fully evacuated, extreme measures were being undertaken in an attempt to save the town. While Unified Command, Forestry, Town of High Level and Mackenzie County were all working together in the same room, Forestry's Incident Management team were proposing an extremely bold protection measure.

"They came to me and said 'you know we think we need to burn out some forest,'" said Schmidt. "You had to visualize that the fire is going from southeast up to northwest and it's scooting across the town and the bottom south end of town. We knew it's just a matter of time before that wind is going to change, and if that wind changed, now this 30 km-long flank of the fire is going to turn into a 30 km-long head of a fire, that's going to point right to town. Our only option really was to take out that chunk of forest before it had a chance to have a wind shift and start heading towards us. Take it out under our terms. The only other option is to hope and pray it doesn't wind shift, and when it does, we fight it off as it reaches the border of town and I don't really like that option. So, let's burn it out."

By May 24, firefighters had used this controlled burn technique to create a containment boundary along Highway 35 south of High Level, Highway 58 west of High Level and the fire perimeter. Jared Snyder and the team at Tim Hortons were among the people witnessing a huge plume of smoke approximately 1 km from their restaurant, which they initially believed to be *The Chuckegg Creek Wildfire*.

"We later learned that was totally intentional," said Snyder. "It was impressive to be watching out this window, because there were dozens of helicopters in the line where they didn't want to burn. The folks would come in they'd be just covered in ash and dirt and you could tell that they were working hard. A lot of people drove 10-12-15 hours even in their fire trucks like from places like Penhold or Hannah or Turner Valley, which are all in southern Alberta, coming up here to help us out."

A look at the controlled burn operation in High Level, as well as the aftermath as seen beside the town walking trail. First photo supplied by the Snyder family, and trail photo by Matthew Marcone.

At Sunscape Gardens just north of Town, ashes were raining down from the sky.

"It wasn't just ashes, it was chunks of wood," said Alexandra Barreira. "Thankfully not hot but they were just pieces that you would find in a fire pit, after you've had a good fire, you know? They littered the deck and hit the top of the greenhouse. It was actually dark in here because of the amount of ashes and soot and stuff that came down."

This forced the Barreira family to begin moving everything away from their buildings and trees, mow all their grass and wet down the entire area.

"We fireproofed our home, fireproofed our property, put more irrigation in the greenhouses, kept watering, kept fertilizing, kept planting, because we were always hoping that it's only going to be a couple days, then it was a week, ok it'll be next week, it just kept going," said Barreira. "And I couldn't just walk away. I know people around here that when it was a voluntary evacuation they just left. I couldn't do that. My livelihood is here."

According to Schmidt, the long days were now beginning to take their toll on emergency responders in particular.

"I could see the toll it was taking on our firefighters," said Schmidt. "We're working super long days, like I'm talking 18 hours a day. I think it was about day three or four; we were doing briefings in the morning. This whole fire station from front to back was full of firefighters for briefings every morning and every night. And I started to realize I haven't talked to my own crew just one-on-one in like three days, because you just get into this mode of 'what's the next step, we're going to do this, going to do that.'"

Shortly after, High Level's Fire Department gathered behind Town Hall for a check-in.

"There's a few tears," said Schmidt. "And I said to them, 'you know we're going to get through this. I want to make sure you guys are doing ok, and have you had time to talk to your families? Make sure you talk to them and let them know that we're doing fine, and that everybody is here with one common goal and that's to make sure this town is still standing at the end of the day.'"

However that outcome remained far from certain.

High Level Fire Department meeting during the evacuation of town. Photo by Josh Lambert.

"I can't remember what night of the week it was but my wife called me, we were trying to FaceTime each other every night," said Schmidt. "She's like how's it going with you? When are we coming home, when is this going to be over [and] when do we come back?' And all I could say is 'I don't know.' She says 'well is everything going to be ok?' and I'm like, 'I just can't tell you.'"

Reinforcements continued arriving from Canada Task Force to help take over EOC operations and Incident Command Operations from the group.

"After a week those people had worked really quite hard, so there were a few of them that were pretty burnt out even after the first four to five days," said McAskile. "Our first goal once we were left in the EOC was to find out who had left town, where they were, what their needs were, did they have shelter, did they have food, did they have their meds, and were their pets taken care of? We said right off the bat that we had to make sure we were communicating on a regular basis to make sure people knew what was going on, what we were doing, and sharing pictures from inside town, because of course the rumors were flying around."

Schmidt says his phone was buzzing continuously during this period and that he was unable to answer 90 per cent of his messages.

"I felt I owed them some sort of explanation of what was going on, so I sat up in my bed with no power and I was typing away on my phone," said Schmidt. "Then I had taken pictures through the days, so I added some pictures and said 'because there's lots of rumors going around – like there's embers landing in town and things are burning up – I thought I need to set the record straight. No. We're still here. We're not out of the woods, but you can be guaranteed we are spending every minute of every day trying to figure this out.' And it spread like crazy."

As more resources continued pouring into the region, firefighters were working hard to contain their fire perimeter to the southwest of Town, being able to take advantage of lighter winds.

South of High Level, Paddle Prairie Council declared a local state of emergency on May 25 at 5:18 p.m., and issued an evacuation order on May 26. The weather conditions led to yet another increase in activity from *The Chuckegg Creek Wildfire*, which was now 107,000 hectares in size.

CHAPTER 5

The Calm Before The Storm & Paddle Prairie Metis Settlement

The weather forecast today will continue to bring hotter temperatures and winds will be light out of the southwest. This in result will help firefighters to continue to make good progress on the fire. The last recorded size is approximately 130,000 hectares.

Heavy equipment continues to make good progress on sections of the fire perimeter. Alberta Wildfire firefighters in conjunction with municipal firefighters, along with air support from helicopters and airtankers continue to work hard to contain the fire. The main area of spread remains away from town. There have been no homes or businesses damaged to date but the threat remains.

The High Level Fire Department and other municipal firefighters have set up sprinklers on the southwest and northwest side of town. In addition, structural protection has been completed on Mackenzie County homes southeast of High Level, Tolko and Norbord.

Structural firefighters have also been taking preventive measures on homes. This includes removing debris from yards, removing patio furniture from decks and other flammable material. There are 168 structural firefighters that continue to establish and maintain structural protection on homes in the Town of High Level and on other critical values at risk within Mackenzie County. Alberta Wildfire has 420 firefighters along with 28 helicopters on this fire. There are more resources arriving daily.

ATCO has restored power supply and is supporting normal operations to Mackenzie County, Town of High Level, La Crete, Fort Vermilion & Dene Tha' First Nation. ATCO has secured large-scale backup generators that can be drawn on to provide power to communities, if needed.

Alberta Agriculture and Forestry High Level Wildfire Update: May 28, 2019

As solid progress was being made battling *The Chuckegg Creek Wildfire,* many were hoping that a re-entry into Town would be happening in the near future. Highway 35 remained closed in both directions, along with Highway 58 west of High Level.

"At one point the fire was 25 km away from High Level to the west and we were planning reentry," said Schmidt. "And the fire just does this little hook on Watt Mountain and comes back towards town and pops up 12 km west of town. We had taken sprinklers down in town thinking we were going to get people home and the fire was out of out of danger here. Then all of a sudden it grows life again and does its thing. It was almost like people got deflated because we were all talking about bringing people home and then all of a sudden, the fire bursts to life again."

"We weren't just covering High Level at that point," Schmidt continued. "We had Mackenzie County in position south to Norbord and towards Bushe River, and we were covering all these lower areas. It was starting to get bigger and bigger. You'd think after a few days or so we should have this, but we didn't. Every time we thought we had something, the fire just threw another curveball at us. It was pretty crazy."

It would be the erratic wind shifts in winds that posed the biggest challenge for emergency responders.

"The winds are circling around, even [Alberta] Wildfire and Forestry couldn't tell us," said Mayor McAteer. "They were experiencing something that they said they've never experienced, with both the winds and everything else that was happening in our region. The winds were unprecedented. Every morning I'd get up and I think 'please don't blow today,' you just see and then by like 10 o'clock, it was just full blown."

Paddle Prairie Metis Settlement is situated 72 km south of High Level and 200 km north of Peace River. It is one of eight Metis Settlements in Alberta and is inhabited by approximately 700 community members, 215 homes and a massive land area of 429,671 acres. It is populated by a wide variety of wildlife and boreal vegetation, with hunting, fishing, trapping and gathering being a way of life for many settlement members.

Between May 12 and May 28, there was not a single mention of *The Chuckegg Creek Wildfire's* potential threat to Paddle Prairie Metis Settlement in official updates posted by Alberta Agriculture and Forestry, despite a voluntary evacuation in the Settlement on May 22 and a mandatory evacuation by Paddle Prairie Council on May 26.

Initially, the fire was not believed to be a threat to the community, until it managed to cross the fireguard north of the Settlement (Peace River at Tompkins Landing) as a result of a radical wind shift to the southeast. This fuelled an area of dense forest that led straight into Paddle Prairie.

By May 28, *The Chuckegg Creek Wildfire* was 20 km from the Settlement, roaring at 130,000 hectares, and becoming a serious threat to local homes and infrastructure.

"There was nothing we could do just to stop this fire from doing what it wanted to do," said Schmidt. "Cat guards, air tankers, helicopters, fire trucks, whatever it was, the fire just kind of keeps doing what it wants to when it gets that large."

As the fire began making its run towards Paddle Prairie, Forestry called for reinforcements to help with the burning activities in the area.

"We wanted to try and guard off those power poles and light off some of the meadow, grassy, forested area, to try and slow the fire down so it doesn't advance into Paddle Prairie," said Schmidt. "We got six more trucks, sprinkler trailers some crews and we shipped south. I got in a helicopter with one of our division supervisors from Clearwater County. We got up in a helicopter, flew Paddle Prairie and made a plan, flew over each house and as we were flying over, we could see that the fire crews from High Level, Grand Prairie, Slave Lake, all these crews together are working as one team, going from house to house fire smarting."

Fire crews work to protect infrastructure in Paddle Prairie Metis Settlement. Photo by Jarrett Austin.

In response to the crisis, Mackenzie County issued an evacuation order for people staying in the La Crete Ferry Campground – east to Range Road 164 and north/south of

Highway 697 – on May 29. That afternoon, it was becoming clear that the fire would reach Paddle Prairie.

"We landed at this one house where the crews were fire smarting," said Schmidt. "We pulled out our map after we drew all over it in the helicopter, and made our plan to the crews. We said 'sprinkle these homes in the direct path, and just keep working south down the highway because this fire is going to arrive here this afternoon.'"

"We kept in contact regarding the fire situation and we were always assured it wasn't going to be a threat to us," said Dean Ducharme, Paddle Prairie's Director of Emergency Operations. "They told us that on numerous occasions and then the fire jumped the guard and just travelled. The 29th, I would say about 2:30 in the afternoon, We knew we were in trouble. We knew it was coming in and there was nothing we can do. To me we were given insufficient time warning [to evacuate]. I was just worried about getting everyone out of here. They tried to start saving on the north end and work their way to the Hamlet."

The main evacuation route for Paddle Prairie members was south on Highway 35 to Highway 2 toward Grande

Prairie, and the Settlement's team at the Administration Building coordinated buses for members without vehicles.

"So the road is closed because the fire is across the highway and the lines are down, and they said 'it's dark there because of the smoke, there's no way we can land,'" said Schmidt. "So, they were on their own. It was six or seven trucks and some sprinkle trailers and about 30 firefighters from 3-4-5 communities including our own. And they went all night, so I stayed up until 1 a.m. listening to the radio."

"I think it was my most nervous time," continued Schmidt. "As the person in charge of structure protection for that incident, listening to these crews, do what we call bumping and running to each house, and the fire would come up to a house and they would stay there defend it. They would spray the house, spray the fire around it, the fire will go around and they move to the next house. House after house after house, and we knew we lost structures because we were hearing them on the radios, 'Chief this house is on fire' and Evan would call back to him and say 'just leave it. There's nothing we can do. We have small amount of resources, don't fight the house. Save what you can save.' And they went on all night."

Ducharme described the feeling of seeing *The Chuckegg Creek Wildfire* enter Paddle Prairie Metis Settlement, which on this night destroyed 14 member homes and great deal of other structural property.

"We could see that fire just rolling away on top of the tree lines," said Ducharme. "It wasn't even on the ground it was so fierce and powerful, with just the winds and everything it just carried. It burned and unbelievable space in a short amount of time. The most northerly houses that we have over there, they were probably all burnt within five minutes of each other. To us, that was where the eye of the fire came through. It was just unreal like we can't even explain it. I have never in my whole 40 some years of living in Paddle, I have never experienced a disaster like this and nobody else has. It is unreal. Just this force of the fire… nothing was going to go stop it and that fire was going to do whatever it wanted."

One of 14 homes is destroyed in Paddle Prairie Metis Settlement from The Chuckegg Creek Wildfire. Despite losing the homes, many others were saved as a result of a collaborative effort from firefighters, including 30-40 members in Paddle Prairie who fought the fire for over a month. A rebuilding effort is underway, as Paddle Prairie secured a loan from the Metis Settlements General Council for $3 million to replace the burnt houses.

Ironically, a disaster of this magnitude can also have the effect of bringing out the best in people.

"We were successful in saving at least 10 more houses along with the structural fire group from different fire departments throughout Alberta," said Ducharme. "It was something that the guys... they were just like me of course.

You come home and try to save your community. We are so close knit and we are so small that everybody knows everybody."

"There were about as many community members down there as firefighters," said Schmidt. "I think it was about 30, and they were the water truck guys and people who ran the community center, and the store owner and so many other people down there that just stayed. And we couldn't have fought it off without them. The whole community banded together to save the town."

"Our guys went down there thinking they were on a shift and got stuck for 30 hours," Schmidt continued. "They got bottled water from the store, beef jerky and whatever they could to keep themselves fed. They laid their heads down on the floor in the community center and the community cooked for them, and brought water in. And the water truck guys were filling up water trucks and bringing water to our crews to fill their trucks, and then just one thing after another. I mean the firefighters are a huge part of it but they couldn't have done it without that community banding together and making it happen. It was a tough day but I think it could've been so much worse."

After fighting *The Chuckegg Creek Wildfire* for two weeks and being able to protect local infrastructure, suddenly 14 homes were incinerated overnight.

"It was a kick in the ass, that's really what it was," said Schmidt. "You know we've been doing so good up to that point and I took it pretty hard. I was feeling pretty good about myself by but week two in Paddle Prairie, I was like 'you know this fire just did it again.'"

Some members of Paddle Prairie remain upset by the response and are still trying to process exactly what happened. Schmidt said the real story is how the community banded together.

"We told the story that these people fought hard and this is what they did," said Schmidt. "And the press picked up on the Paddle fight and did some interviews of our crews, and we kind of changed the message a little bit. We were telling the real story of what happened, how those group of 30 people made such a difference in that community."

CHAPTER 6
Fire Growth & Residents Return to High Level

Firefighters, heavy equipment, and aircraft are focusing on establishing containment in priorities areas. The fire continues to be active with growth on the west side today. Structural and wildland firefighters continue to work around Paddle Prairie to protect values. On the east side of the Peace River by Tompkins Landing, fire guard lines have been completed from the agricultural land to the Peace River with structural and municipal firefighters extinguishing hot spots along the fire perimeter to limit spread. Air tankers and bucketing helicopters are assisting ground operations as possible, but thick smoke continues to limit visibility on parts of the fire.

Firefighters continue to consolidate containment along Highways 35 and 58. Heavy equipment is building fireguards to the north of High Level to limit further spread of the fire towards Hutch Lake. The forecast tomorrow anticipates dry conditions with winds prevailing from the west and southwest, with gusts up to 35 km/hour. A <u>red flag weather warning</u> has been issued, with the *potential for extreme fire behaviour tomorrow. While today saw scattered precipitation and thundershowers across parts of the fire that can dampen fire activity and aid suppression efforts, any return of warm and dry weather can revive fire behaviour. The last recorded size is approximately 265,925 hectares. Alberta Wildfire has 452 firefighters, along with 112 structural firefighters. There are 28 helicopters.*

Alberta Agriculture and Forestry High Level Wildfire Update: June 1, 2019

County of Northern Lights declared a State of Local Emergency on May 30, issuing a mandatory evacuation order for residents in the Keg River and Carcajou areas.

Firefighters would also utilize winds coming from the east to conduct a successful controlled burn-off by the Boyer Towers east towards Highway 35. This was done to protect the towers by eliminating *The Chuckegg Creek Wildfire's* source of fuel in this area.

On June 2, an eight-hour evacuation alert was issued for residents in Mackenzie County east of High Level in areas north and south of the Peace River, including Fort Vermilion, La Crete, Beaver First Nation, Boyer River and Child Lake

Reserves. Mandatory evacuations remained in place throughout parts of Mackenzie County, and all of Paddle Prairie, High Level and Steen River.

Residents of Town of High Level finally get the news they've been waiting for on June 3; that the evacuation order is lifted and it is safe to come home. They remained on evacuation alert.

"It was just pretty much constant the whole time," said McAskile. "Just the amount of decisions that had to be made, the things that had to be organized as things went on. We brought 4000 people back into town, 750 back on the reserve and a few hundred south of town. It was really hard for those first few days to convince some of the more nervous people that the town was safe, that what we were experiencing was smoke or even ash from a fire that was a considerable distance away."

Staff at Town of High Level quickly learned that it is a lot easier to evacuate the Town than it is to bring people back home.

"I didn't realize that the hospital needs to be completely cleaned and grocery stores need to get out all their old stock and add their new stock, and then they have to have health inspections and the gas stations have to be ready," said Mayor McAteer. "We have to be ready to receive the people."

"This little girl brought me those flowers and I still have them, and I started to cry after she said 'thank you for saving our town,'" McAteer continued. "That was the best feeling that I've had throughout this whole fire thing, because I think I just detached and did what we had to do. I just listened to the experts, and when they said 'I have a good feeling,' I listened. Everything was decided in consultation with council, with the Dene Tha and with the County, so it was a good feeling to know that our region was standing together at that point."

Residents of Town of High Level return home after the mandatory evacuation ends on June 3, 2019. Photo by Leslie Snyder.

By this time, national press were well in tune to what was happening throughout the region.

"We set up a big flag on the Fire Hall, and Slave Lake Fire Service left us another huge flag that we hung from our ladder truck to welcome people as they came in," said Schmidt. "We had people crying as they were driving by us and waving and honking, and then we attended a barbecue at the arena. We were meeting people there, giving hugs, and some of our firefighters families are coming back and they're crying. It was an emotional day bringing everybody back, but in the back of my head I couldn't help but think 'we're not done yet. We've still got work to do.'"

While Paddle Prairie Metis Settlement continued to be evacuated, Mackenzie County's eight-hour evacuation alert was lifted for most of the region. County of Northern Lights also rescinded their evacuation order for Keg River and Carcajou residents on June 5, along with all people located west of Range Road 185, north and south of Highway 697 and La Crete Ferry Campground. Things finally seemed to be heading in the right direction.

"The Chuckegg fire was such a massive natural occurrence," said Cardinal. "We never thought it could grow to the size that it was. So when we were done the two weeks of evacuations, we thought the Chuckegg was slowing down, but it was just taking a break."

CHAPTER 7
Mandatory Evacuation in La Crete

Due to no significant rainfall and gusty winds, the fire saw an increase in fire activity on the southwest, west and east side of the Chuckegg Creek fire today. Firefighters carried out controlled burn operations as conditions allowed on the southeast side removing fuels adjacent to the fire perimeter. Plans for a controlled burn on the west side of the fire are still underway as heavy equipment works towards establishing a guard in preparation for the burn.

Bucketing helicopters continue to assist firefighters on the ground as possible. Firefighters continue to work around Paddle Prairie to extinguish hotspots and will be utilizing infrared scans to assist with identifying priority areas. Firefighters are continuing to cut helipads on the west side of the fire to gain access in priority areas. Dozer guard has been completed from the Boyer River to the Peace River to limit fire spread to the east and continues to be established in the south. Alberta Wildfire has 785 firefighters and personnel. With 42 helicopters and 135 pieces of heavy equipment.

Alberta Agriculture and Forestry High Level Wildfire Update: June 8, 2019

In the lead-up to the evacuation of La Crete and other parts of Mackenzie County, *The Chuckegg Creek Wildfire* continued growing in size, although temporarily in the right direction. By June 11, evacuation alerts were lifted in Town of High Level, Bushe River and the Mackenzie County rural areas north and south of High Level.

The area west of Blues Creek and Blue Hills road (Range Road 180) – north and south of Highway 697 – remained under evacuation alert.

The smoke was less intense by 11 a.m. on June 12, allowing firefighters to receive much needed air support from helicopters with buckets. Flare-ups remained active on the south, east and west sides of the fire, and ashes were reported to be landing south of High Level.

Nonetheless, *The Chuckegg Creek Wildfire* appeared to no longer be an immediate threat to Town of Manning, Keg River or Carajou areas, with evacuation alerts being lifted in these boundaries as well.

"And then of course the world changed and the fire jumped down to Blue Hills area," said Racher. "And this created a whole new dynamic around the community of La Crete."

La Crete is a predominantly Mennonite community located 135 km southeast of High Level, thriving on an abundant agricultural and forestry industry. The Hamlet is home to approximately 3,400 people, many of whom still use the Low German and High German languages that remain spoken in Germany. The surrounding rural areas of La Crete make up approximately 8,000 people, all of whom were about to cross paths with *The Chuckegg Creek Wildfire*.

On June 17, the fire was 10 km west of La Crete and approximately 6 km north of the Boyer River Cell Tower. It was expected to move throughout the night with 15-20 km/hour winds from the southwest, forcing La Crete to evacuate by 11 p.m. on short notice.

"We were told by Forestry 'you got about eight hours,'" said Racher. "The fire's heading towards La Crete at the river and we knew prior to this that it would jump the river. It's a quarter of a mile wide but it will jump the river very quickly.

We had to evacuate La Crete and then the fire was anticipated to jump down what we call the pines area and Sand Hills area. Now we had to make a real big decision of how do we evacuate La Crete and where do we do that? So the crews of people that we had were just trying to stay ahead of all news."

Relief appeared to have come in the form of rainfall, however to *The Chuckegg Creek Wildfire*, a little rainfall meant absolutely nothing.

"We were criticized, 'what in the heck are you doing 11 o'clock and evacuating the town of 3,400 people,' but we don't have that privilege of making those life and death decisions for people," said Racher. "We have to err on the side of caution and we'll do that every day of the week. Yes it was inconvenient for people but we got them out of there."

By this point there were 851 firefighters and personnel, 153 pieces of heavy equipment and 52 helicopters working on the fire, which was now approaching 300,000 hectares in size. Approximately 7,100 people registered at reception centres throughout Alberta.

Additionally, evacuation alerts were back in place throughout the region. A controlled back burn took place along the Peace River, where firefighters reduced the risk of the fire spotting across the river and into Blue Hills.

Tensions remained high among the evacuees, as was the case in High Level and in Paddle Prairie. Among the La Crete residents opting to stay behind was Jake Fehr – CEO of Canwest Air – who would be taking daily aerial photos and posting on social media to ensure people knew their community was safe. He would receive thousands of messages thanking him for these pictures.

One of the many aerial photos taken by Jake Fehr during the mandatory evacuation in La Crete on June 18, 2019. This photo was made available to the public via Fehr's Facebook page.

"When the fire started getting close to La Crete, we had a full camp set up there for our first Nations neighbors, Paddle Prairie and anybody else who wanted to use it," said Racher. "That of course became a dangerous spot, so we moved that camp to Fort [Vermilion]. Fort always seemed to be out of real danger zone, so we set up a massive camp there to accommodate the elderly, the children and families. We started getting fairly good at organizing a small temporary city."

With the help of Mike McMann and the Fort Vermilion School Division, Fort Vermilion again became an important nearby relief spot for evacuees.

"For many of them to just travel to another section of the region, it doesn't happen very often," said McMann. "And it was interesting. We kind of joked about it but when we started to set up camp in Fort Vermilion, the kids always affectionately call Alberta housing the Bronx in Fort Vermillion. So then when we evacuated La Crete, we put up camping behind for the public and we called that East LA. It was the first time La Crete was a suburb of Fort Vermillion and those two communities don't always spend a lot of time with each other in an intimate setting like that too, so it was really cool."

"And then we had a whole bunch of teachers down at Central Office and we called that Central Park," McMann continued. "And then we had another camp set up at St Mary's, which we didn't use fortunately. We called that Upper Manhattan, had a little New York City there. There were a group of us that were just having fun with what we were doing, and committed to serving the people that we needed to serve. It wasn't about us. We just became servants of what we needed to do in the moment. Not knowing when it was going to end, that was hardest part."

Two days into the La Crete evacuation, winds were gusting 35-45 km/hour. The smoke remained heavy due to burning in peaty soils and windrows. Fortunately the fire still had not crossed the river.

"We are concerned about the potential for the fire to cross the river or spot across into this area," stated a June 19 update from Alberta Agriculture and Forestry. "In addition to strong overnight winds, the winds from tomorrow are predicted to be N/NW 25 to 35 gusting to 50 km/hour. This area will be under careful scrutiny."

CHAPTER 8

Paddle Prairie and La Crete Residents Return Home

Mother Nature helped firefighters out today by sending rain to most parts of the wildfire. Between noon and 3 pm today Tompkins Landing received 10 mm of rain, Rocky Lane received 1.5 mm, near the TOHL received 3 mm, and the west part of the fire received no rain.

The rain and the increased humidity thwarted firefighters plans for ignition today and likely for tomorrow as well. Instead, firefighters made good progress working on the perimeter of the fire in all areas, concentrating on hotspots along Hwy 58, and on the spot fire on the east side of the Peace River. Burning is very deep in these areas.

The forecast for tomorrow is for a high of 21 degrees, humidity at 30-35%, winds E/SE 10-15 and a chance of thundershowers. Sunday, Monday and Tuesday all have rain in the forecast. Under these conditions there should not be any significant fire growth for the next five to seven days.

The fire is now 331, 245 hectares. There are 816 firefighters and personnel, 52 helicopters, 153 pieces of heavy equipment.

Alberta Agriculture and Forestry High Level Wildfire Update: June 21, 2019

As residents of La Crete remained evacuated, a huge sigh of relief comes over Paddle Prairie Metis Settlement, as their mandatory evacuation order is finally lifted on June 20 at 1 p.m., prompting an emotional return to the community. We were privileged enough to be there and witness many smiles, tears, and powerful sense of unity as members checked back in at the Communi-Plex.

"Some people were gone 33 days," said Ducharme. "The longest ones were people with respiratory illnesses, little babies and the elders. We had a lot of help from the other agencies who are helping us especially Alberta Emergency Response. We've had everyone, the whole northern Alberta, people south of us, everywhere, the whole Alberta stepped up and gave us help one way or another. Like it's overwhelming for me, and still we are still getting it today."

Several individual and corporate donors contributed money and resources during the evacuation. In addition, the

Metis Settlements General Council secured a loan for $3 million for Paddle Prairie to begin work on rebuilding the lost homes, which were nearly replaced in their entirety by December 2019.

A look at the side of Marvin and Lena Parenteau's newly rebuilt Samlan Homes Trailer, which was made possible through the ongoing recovery efforts in Paddle Prairie. Photo by Matthew Marcone.

"The first time we got emotional was actually doing the drive by myself and seeing the devastation because I've hunted there," said Ducharme. "I have lived here all my life, so I am accustomed to seeing what is there, and then when you go there and see what's going on, it's devastating. You look at how many houses, all the forest we lost and all the animals."

In total, Paddle Prairie lost approximately 35 per cent of their land base to *The Chuckegg Creek Wildfire,* and the Settlement is living through an on-going tragedy impacting hunting, fishing, trapping, community programs, and overall sustainability. They also lost their campground, with many members losing animals including chickens, rabbits, cats and dogs. These are among the many mental health and trauma related issues stemming from the wildfire.

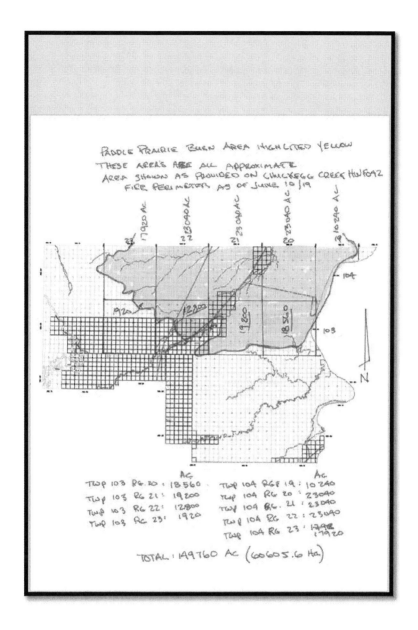

Paddle Prairie lost 35 per cent of its land and 14 homes to the Chuckegg Creek Wildfire as of June 10, 2019, causing a major disruption to the Settlement's way of life.

"There has been good stuff that came out of this," said Ducharme. "We saved the Hamlet, as a community it made us a lot stronger. It brought unity to us. It brought hope, and seeing all the outside support in every way was special as well."

Meanwhile the battle to save La Crete continued to the north. By June 22, there were 1,150 firefighters, 46 helicopters and 311 pieces of heavy equipment working to contain the fire, which was now over 331,000 hectares. Crews were working aggressively and directly on the fire line.

"In the area between Highway 35 and the Peace River, dozers worked to put a guard in along the front of the fire," stated a June 22 update from Alberta Agriculture and Forestry. "Crews followed, with pumps and laying hose along the cleared line to contain the fire. Crews will use these dozer lines to work from, extinguishing fire along the perimeter and then working their way inwards. Other crews continued work on the spot fire across the River, working diligently to extinguish all hotspots and smoldering areas. More crews worked the north and west sides of the fire while others concentrated on the hot spots along Highway 58.

Under these conditions we do not expect the fire to grow for the next several days."

The evacuation for La Crete was officially lifted on June 24 at 2 p.m., allowing 8,104 residents to return to the Hamlet and surrounding area. They managed to avoid a major tragedy; although they too are witness to a remarkable event unlike anything they've been a part of.

"La Crete has never been evacuated ever, so was this the best we could do in six hours?" asked Racher. "That was the big question, and by golly we did. Again it was all the efforts from RCMP, our staff, [and our] School Board. It went very well and when we moved everybody back in we were prepared. We knew we could do it, the people knew they could do it, so you would think it was an exercise, but it was a life and death exercise."

"We didn't have a choice," he continued. "We had to find 'Ok this isn't working and how do we make it work' and it was awesome. People were high-stressed, there was a lot of tension but I didn't see any people trying to hold on to power here or there. We just gave up our egos and got together. Councillors were literally cleaning toilets, serving food, and they really came together. They were like soldiers, and that's kind of how you have to get the momentum going in an emergency like that."

Councillor Cameron Cardinal said he felt an immense sense of pride as a volunteer during this period; making sure people were safe and comfortable throughout the evacuations. It also led to unexpected friendships from older rivalries.

"I believe everything bad that happens, there's always a positive end result," said Cardinal. "And I believe that we made some lifelong relationships with the Dene Tha.' I was introduced Councillor Shane Providence, and it was his first time and my first time on Council. We didn't even really talk about politics, or our roles as councilors in our communities. We just made friendships. And with the two weeks that the Dene Tha' spent with us, we made lifelong relationships that we normally would never get to build."

"How we saw the Dene Tha' from an everyday standpoint to how we see them now, they're just like us," Cardinal continued. "As a region we grew together. We know that if another disaster like this comes, and I hope it doesn't, we know that we can stand beside each other shoulder to shoulder and get the task done."

Chief of Dene Tha' First Nation James Ahnassay also remained in the thick of the decision making process. He witnessed multiple evacuations in the Dene Tha' communities of Bushe, Chateh and Meander River. A separate wildfire also caused the evacuation of nearby Steen River.

"It was almost like nature attacking us from all sides," said Chief Ahnassay. "The fire was in a unique situation here because it involved multiple communities. It started off a small fire but then it spread out to quite the largest I suppose in the recent history, so we took it upon ourselves to be involved with the other committees like Town of High Level, and also the Municipality County of Mackenzie. By doing that, it really helped because we were able to get information from one source and be able to make joint decisions when the evacuations should happen or not."

Mayor McAteer also said she has become closer with Chief Ahnassay and the Dene Tha' as a result of *The Chuckegg Creek Wildfire.*

"We're working in tandem now to do some projects and it's been amazing," said McAteer. "I wish that people down south could see this."

CHAPTER 9

The Chuckegg Creek Wildfire: Being Held

Thanks to the incredibly hard work from thousands of firefighters and support staff, specifically the High Level Forest Area staff, local contractors, business owners, structural firefighting teams from over 30 communities in Alberta and firefighters from across the world, the Chuckegg Creek wildfire is now listed as Being Held (BH). This means that given the current and forecast weather conditions and resources, this wildfire is not anticipated to grow past expected boundaries.

The Chuckegg Creek wildfire is truly an international effort. Firefighters from Alberta, Saskatchewan, British Columbia, Ontario, Northwest Territories, New Brunswick, Nova Scotia, Prince Edward Island, Quebec, Idaho, Oregon, Montana, California, Colorado, Washington and South Africa made their way to the High Level area to offer support. We can't thank you enough! Last recorded size: 351,856 hectares

Alberta Agriculture and Forestry High Level Wildfire Update: July 25, 2019

At its peak, *The Chuckegg Creek Wildfire* was roaring across the province at over 351,800 hectares in size, prompting a truly incredible worldwide response. The fire perimeter was larger than 610 km around; roughly the equivalent of driving a return trip from Edmonton to Calgary! It is difficult to describe the sheer size and power of this wildfire, which continues to test an entire region physically, mentally and emotionally.

Firefighters pose beside the Town of High Level Fire Department. Photo supplied by Rodney Schmidt.

Dan Williams, Member of the Legislative Assembly of Alberta for Peace River, said he was tasked with making sure evacuees had the financial support they needed.

"Had they left in a rush and didn't grab everything that they needed, we wanted to make sure they were still continuing to get by," said Williams, "A lot of folks are out of work at that time. The whole region up here is resource intensive. If you don't have access to the land, if you're not working on it, if you're not involved in that in some way, you're often in economic loss."

A common thread among community members throughout the region – who stayed behind during mandatory evacuation orders – were the remarks regarding how nothing can prepare a person for a natural disaster of this scale.

"I think you just have to do it," said McMann. "You just have to get in there and whatever job's closest to you, that's what you do."

"This fire and this event that occurred here, brought a whole new priority to what you're doing," said Morad. "It wasn't just, 'I hope your steak was done well and I hope you enjoyed your stay.' It's like, 'I hope your rest is sound so you can save our town.' That's a whole other level of purpose for your job, and it was really, really fulfilling day in and day out."

Surviving a natural disaster of this magnitude has also given many people a newfound sense of confidence, as Racher described regarding the team at Mackenzie County.

"All of our projects were stopped dead for two months, where that is normally where we do our business, build roads, [and] fix things," said Racher. "It was all over, now we're getting into winter, so we're going to have a few projects carried over next year. Mackenzie County was heavily relied on throughout this whole event and we never once asked for anything in return. So in that sense I'm very proud of this group because they set the pride showboating aside and we got down to business. We know we can do anything now."

Williams said that the real story behind *The Chuckegg Creek Wildfire* is one of unity.

"It's been an example of the Northern communities fighting hard and coming together," said Williams. "We saw it in La Crete. We saw it in High Level. We saw it in all the different reserves, the entire Beaver [First Nation]. We saw it in Paddle Prairie with the Settlement. We saw it down in Manning as well with that Battle Complex Fire just south of here. And over and over again if I saw one thing coming through is that the north being strong and free is going to make sure that it fights hard for itself. I was really impressed with that. I couldn't be more proud of all the different work. My own brother's a forest fire fighter who's fighting in the Battle Complex Fire. All those men and women who are fighting, I'm really, really impressed with that and all the community coming together."

There has always been a deep appreciation for firefighters in the north given the high vulnerability to wildfires. However, *The Chuckegg Creek Wildfire* of 2019 has taken this to an entirely new level.

"I can't walk down the sidewalk, even two or three months after the fire, without somebody coming up to me and wanting to share a story, say thank you or just ask how we're doing," said Schmidt. "And it means the world to us. It really does. I can't say how much it means because it keeps us going. We've got so much work to do."

This little known region of Northern Alberta had suddenly found itself making major national and international headlines. One business in particular seeing a major impact from this is Raye Smith-Knox, Owner at Raye's Signs in High Level.

"We started out to think we'll raise a few t-shirts," said Smith-Knox on their *Together We Stand* clothing line. "That turned into, 'what if we got hats, what if we got hoodies?' And here we are now and it's exploded on us, and it just kept going and going and far exceeding expectations. We keep setting new goals."

Raye's Signs were able to make a $24,042.22 donation to High Level Fire Department as a result of revenues generated from the idea.

"We picked the black circle because it's circle surrounding our area, all the way from Rainbow Lake, over to La Crete, up to Steen River, down to Paddle Prairie, all encompassed all in one or in that circle," said Smith-Knox. "Together we stand as a whole area. That's how we came up with this."

Together We Stand gear is being sported from Vancouver all the way to Newfoundland. Photo by Jordan Maskell.

"So from one side of our country to the other," said Smith-Knox. "That's pretty phenomenal. Once the people involved see this, they have to talk about their experience, tell you whether they were living here before, and have family members here, whatever it may be. RCMP have come in here and bought hats, so we hear their stories from wherever they're from across the province. We've heard so many stories of the uniqueness of it all and the signs that are welcoming people home, and still you see them up there today and there's always somebody that's got a story about it."

RCMP Corporal Sue Harvey – who lives in High Level with her family and stayed behind during the evacuation order – said that some returning residents are displaying symptoms of Post Traumatic Stress Disorder (PTSD). The scientific evidence has been growing to suggest that some particles – as a result of poor air quality – may be small enough to enter the human brain and cause neuro-inflammation. This can affect a person's mood and cognitive abilities.

"Some of our community members did have to drive through the fire trying to get back from Rainbow [Lake] on the first few days there," said Harvey. "I am a PTSD survivor, and I like to say PTSD warrior and it was hard. It was hard as a first responder here. I've been in the military. I have been first responder for over a decade, and when I go mission ready, I'm mission ready. I take the mission and we go, but this was different because we were at home, but we were on a mission."

For others like Sherry Matthews, *The Chuckegg Creek Wildfire* has made High Level feel more like home than ever before.

"This is home for us," said Matthews. "And seeing all these people when I'm at the supermarket, and they smile, they were smiling at us before but now I feel kind of a different smile. It's a thank you smile and it just means a lot. I don't think about it too much, because I find it hard to really process how good people were to us."

One of the lesser-known and remarkable facts about wildfires is that they have the capability of smoldering underground throughout the winter, with snow acting as an insulator.

"That fire's still there," said Schmidt. "It's not out. Here in Alberta, it's still burning and we don't see it every day because it's just smolders here and a smolders there, but that fire is likely going to smolder through the winter. Not that it's going to pick up and be this roaring monster next spring but our focus now is changing to preparing the community for what wildfire season brings us next year. And that anxiety I think will come with a wildfire on the horizon of town."

Schmidt said that even though High Level did not lose any structures or lives, there remains a healing that needs to take place throughout the region.

"It certainly needs to happen within our department," said Schmidt. "We're going through a time and our firefighters are now trying to process what happened in the last few months, and I think the community needs to process that too. That's probably part of the reason that we have so many people approaching us and asking us questions about what happened. So, I think at the end of the day, what I'm learning from an event like this is even though the town is still here, the community still needs to understand what happened in the fire and how to heal from it, so we're not all worried next year about what's going to happen next."

REFERENCES

- Causes of Wildfires:
  https://wildfire.alberta.ca/reports/activeld.pdf

- Northwest Territories 2014 Wildfire Facts:
  https://www.cbc.ca/news/canada/north/2014-n-w-t-fire-season-report-what-you-need-to-know-1.3061930

- Alberta Agriculture and Forestry Wildfire Updates:
  http://srd.web.alberta.ca/high-level-area-update/all

- Health Effects of Wildfire Smoke
  https://globalnews.ca/news/5336828/health-effects-of-wildfire-smoke-research/

PHOTO AND VIDEO CONTRIBUTORS

- Jordan Maskell
- Matthew Marcone
- Jarrett Austin
- Alexandra Barreira
- Cameron Cardinal
- Josh Lambert
- Angie Mann
- Alexis Maskell
- Dave Peters
- Rodney Schmidt
- Bill Schnarr
- Leslie Snyder
- Town of High Level
- Mackenzie County
- Government of Alberta

SPECIAL THANKS

- Paddle Prairie Metis Settlement
- Mackenzie County
- Town of High Level
- Government of Alberta
- Rodney Schmidt
- Len Racher
- Crystal McAteer
- Clark McAskile
- Alexandra & Tony Barreira
- Mike McMann
- George Fehr
- Jan Welke
- Sherry Matthews
- Angie Mann
- Malcolm Gunson
- Charles LaForge
- Cameron Cardinal

- Melodie Badour
- Tareq Morad
- Leslie, Paul and Jared Snyder
- Dean Ducharme
- Alberta Emergency Management Agency
- Mike Morgan
- James Ahnassay
- Dan Williams
- Raye Smith-Knox
- Sue Harvey
- Lorraine Poitras

Made in the USA
Monee, IL
31 January 2020